Mini Cupcakes

Lorna Fleming

First published in Great Britain 2015

Search Press Limited
Wellwood, North Farm Road,
Tunbridge Wells, Kent TN2 3DR

Text copyright © Lorna Fleming 2015

Photographs by Laura Forrester on location

Photographs and design copyright
© Search Press Ltd 2015

Print ISBN: 978-1-78221-064-1
EPUB ISBN: 978-1-78126-223-8
Mobi ISBN: 978-1-78126-224-5

The Publishers and author can accept no
responsibility for any consequences arising from
the information, advice or instructions given in
this publication.

Readers are permitted to reproduce any of the
items in this book for their personal use, or for
the purposes of selling for charity, free of charge
and without the prior permission of the Publishers.
Any use of the items for commercial purposes is
not permitted without the prior permission of
the Publishers.

Suppliers
If you have difficulty in obtaining any of the
materials and equipment mentioned in this book,
then please visit the Search Press website for
details of suppliers: www.searchpress.com

Printed in China

Dedication

*To my parents for understanding that cake is very
important, and to the one who now finds himself
living in a bakery from morning until midnight.*

Contents

Introduction

The recent cupcake phenomenon started my love of baking. This naturally led to teaching myself how to decorate cakes. Inevitably, eating cupcakes has also become a very important part of my life!

Creating this book seemed a natural step to take to share my passion with others – it enables me to show people how simple decorating a mini cupcake can be. I lead a busy life so time is of the essence, and being able to produce great-looking cupcakes in minimal time is important to me.

I love nothing more than a bold, simple yet stylish design. Mini cupcakes, although small, should still capture these elements; minimum fuss with maximum impact. Remember, a mini cupcake is a tiny canvas on which to work, so do not drown it with complicated design.

The designs I have put together in this book are simple to create in the first instance, and simple to reproduce on a larger scale, without being too fiddly or time-consuming to make. I use simple tools that are used across the different projects, and which are readily available in shops selling cake decorating supplies.

One thing I have learnt from eating many different cupcakes from many different bakeries is that, however good the little masterpiece may look, do not forget that it is there to be eaten. Get the actual taste and texture of the cupcake right, avoid over-baking your cake, and do not swamp your mini delight in heaps of frosting and icing. Less is always more. The decoration is there to add the 'wow factor'!

Within this book there is a design fit for every occasion. Use the designs for inspiration to fit your own special occasion. Combine design elements from a selection of the projects, and play around with different colours to create your own unique display of mini cupcakes.

Tools and materials

You will need many of the basic tools and materials here for the projects in this book:

Mini cupcake cases

Mini muffin tins

Hand-mixer or stand mixer

Weighing scales

Ice cream scoop

Piping bags

Open star piping nozzle (Wilton 1M)

Greaseproof paper, foam pads and **foam cupped drying trays** are useful surfaces on which to dry paste decorations.

For each project you will need a **small paintbrush** to apply the edible glue used to attach pieces of fondant (sugarpaste) and flower paste to each other.

Small non-stick rolling pin This is used for rolling out your paste. A **non-stick work board** makes it easier to roll out the paste without it moving. Place a

non-slip mat underneath to prevent your board from moving.

Cutters, made of plastic or metal, come in various shapes such as ovals, circles, hearts, stars, rabbits and flowers.

A **mini palette knife** is used to release paste from the board.

A **craft knife** is useful for cutting fondant (sugarpaste) and flower paste to shape.

A **stitching wheel tool** can be used to mark and add texture to the paste.

A **ball tool** is used to make indentations and curves, and to frill petals.

Cocktail sticks are used for marking and texturing. **Wooden skewers** are used to wrap flower paste around to make curled ribbon shapes.

Silicone moulds are used to make paste buttons, bows, flowers and bead shapes.

Fondant (sugarpaste) is a sweet, edible sugar dough made from sugar and glucose. **Flower paste** is less sweet than fondant (sugarpaste) but sets much harder.

Nonpareils are a decorative confectionery of tiny balls made of sugar and starch; larger ones are called **edible sprinkles**.

Lustre/blossom dust is used to add colour to flower paste.

Edible glue is used to attach pieces of fondant (sugarpaste) and flower paste to each other.

Edible ink colouring pens are used to draw on fondant (sugarpaste) and flower paste.

Food colouring paste is added to fondant (sugarpaste) and flower paste to change the colour.

White vegetable fat stops the paste from sticking to the board when rolling it out.

Cornflour stops paste from sticking to silicone moulds.

Basic cupcake recipe

Basic vanilla cupcakes

Makes approximately 50 mini cupcakes
50 mini muffin cases (31 x 19mm/1¼ x ¾in)
Mini muffin tins

Ingredients:

110g/4oz unsalted butter, at room temperature

225g/8oz caster sugar

2 large eggs, free-range or organic

275g/9½oz self-raising flour

120ml/4fl oz semi-skimmed milk

1 tsp (5ml) good-quality vanilla extract

Instructions:

1 Preheat the oven to 180°C/160°C (fan)/gas 4 and line a mini muffin tray with cases.

2 Set out all ingredients.

3 In a large mixing bowl, cream the butter and sugar until the mixture is pale and fluffy.

4 Add the eggs, one at a time on a low speed, mixing for a few minutes after each addition.

5 At this point, you should have a liquid mixture. It is important not to mix things too much from this point, as over-mixing can make the gluten (the protein in the flour) tough.

6 Into a separate bowl, sieve the flour.

7 Pour the milk into a jug and add the vanilla extract to it.

8 Add one third of the flour to the creamed mixture and beat well. Pour in one third of the milk and beat again. Repeat these steps until all the flour and milk have been added.

9 Spoon the mixture into the cupcake cases, using an ice cream scoop with a release button (if you have one); this will ensure there is an even amount of mixture in each case. Fill the cases three-quarters full.

10 Bake the cupcakes in the oven for 15–20 minutes. Test the cupcakes at 15 minutes by inserting a cocktail stick. If it comes out clean, they are done. If there is uncooked batter clinging to it, return the cupcakes to the oven for a few more minutes.

11 Remove the cupcakes from the oven and leave to cool for 2 minutes or until cool enough to remove from the muffin tray. Place on a wire rack or kitchen surface to cool.

12 Once completely cooled, ice and decorate the cupcakes.

Vanilla buttercream icing

Enough for approximately 50 mini cupcakes

Ingredients:

250g/9oz unsalted butter, at room temperature

500g/18oz icing sugar

1 tsp (5ml) good-quality vanilla extract

2–4 tbsp (30–60ml) milk, water or double cream

Food colouring paste of your choice

Instructions:

1 Put the butter in a mixer and mix until it becomes slightly paler in colour.

2 Add half the icing sugar to the butter and mix on a low speed. When it is mixed in, scrape down the sides of the bowl.

3 Add the remaining icing sugar, the vanilla and 2 tablespoons (30ml) of milk. Again mix on a low speed to begin with, then turn up to a high speed. Mix until the frosting is light and fluffy. It may be necessary to add another tablespoon of liquid; however, always add with care. Too much liquid and the buttercream will be too runny to pipe, too little liquid and it will be impossible to pipe the buttercream swirls.

4 Colour the buttercream using the food colouring paste.

5 The buttercream is ready to pipe onto the mini cupcakes.

Basic Mini Cupcake

Materials:

Mini cupcakes
Buttercream
Sprinkles

Tools:

Piping bag
Star piping nozzle (Wilton 1M)
Small bowl

Instructions:

1 Take a piping bag and cut off the tip so that when inserted, the piping nozzle will sit half in the bag and half protruding through the end of the bag. If the hole is cut too big, the nozzle will either fall straight out or, when pressure is applied, the buttercream will force it out.

2 Holding the piping bag with one hand or resting it in a large glass, fold back the edges of the bag, opening it out over your hand or over the sides of a glass.

3 Using a spatula, half fill the bag with buttercream. If you overfill the piping bag, it will be too heavy to handle or buttercream will shoot out of the top of the bag when pressure is applied.

4 Unfold the sides of the bag and, using your fingers, work the buttercream down inside the bag and towards the nozzle – this will eliminate some of the air bubbles. Twist the end of the bag to close it, and you are ready to pipe.

5 Grip the twisted end of the piping bag between your thumb and index finger. This hand will act as a squeezing mechanism to push the buttercream out of the bag. Your other hand will act as a stabiliser to guide the nozzle.

6 Squeeze out a small amount of buttercream into a bowl to release any further air bubbles that may have formed.

7 Take a cooled cupcake and place it on your work surface. With the piping bag in a vertical position over the cupcake and the nozzle just touching the outer edge of the cupcake, begin to squeeze the buttercream out through the nozzle.

8 When buttercream appears, raise the nozzle slightly to allow it to disperse. Move the nozzle in a circular motion, while maintaining a constant pressure on the bag.

9 Once the outer edge of the cupcake is covered with buttercream, continue to work in a circular motion towards the centre of the cupcake.

10 Stop squeezing the bag when you reach the centre and, with a short sharp action, lift the nozzle away.

11 Before the buttercream forms a skin, apply some sprinkles. Do this by holding the cupcake in one hand over a bowl to catch any loose sprinkles.

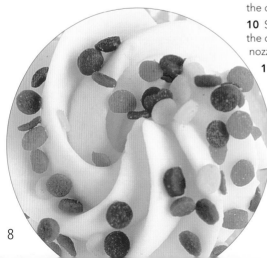

Birthday Boy

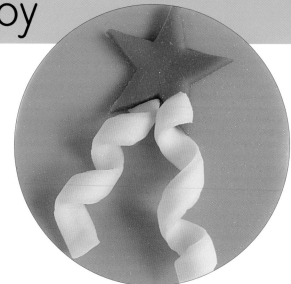

Materials:

Mini cupcakes

Buttercream

Yellow, green and blue fondant (sugarpaste)

Yellow, green and blue flower paste

Edible glue

Tools:

3.5cm (1⅜in) round cutter

Star cutters, several sizes

Small wooden skewers

Foam pad or greaseproof paper

Instructions:

1 Start by making the discs for the decorations to be mounted onto. Take some fondant (sugarpaste) and roll it out on a non-stick work board, to about 2mm (⅛in) in thickness. Cut out circles using the round cutter. Set aside to dry out on greaseproof paper while you make the decorations.

2 To make the stars, roll out the flower paste to 1mm (¹⁄₁₆in) in thickness and, using the cutters, cut out mini stars and large stars. Set them aside to dry on a foam pad or piece of greaseproof paper.

3 To make the spiralled ribbons, start with a small ball of flower paste about the size of a small marble. Roll it out into a sausage shape until you have a long, rope-like piece about 2mm (⅛in) in thickness. Cut into lengths of about 5cm (2in). Wrap each piece around a wooden skewer and set aside to dry for about 10 minutes. Gently remove the spirals from the sticks and rest them on a foam pad to dry.

4 To assemble the cupcake toppers, apply small amounts of edible glue to the decorations and arrange them on the discs. Leave them to dry while you bake, cool and ice the mini cupcakes.

5 Apply the decorated discs to the buttercream-topped cupcakes.

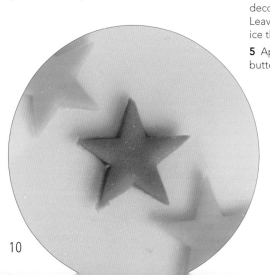

Birthday Girl

Materials:

Mini cupcakes

Buttercream

Yellow and pale blue fondant (sugarpaste)

Yellow and pale blue flower paste

Cornflour

Edible glue

Tools:

Small party dress cutter

Medium petal cutter

Small oval plunger cutter

Silicone bow and flower mould

Silicone pearl bead mould

Foam pad or greaseproof paper

Stitching wheel tool

Craft knife

Instructions:

1 Start by making the dresses. Take some yellow fondant (sugarpaste) and roll it out on a non-stick work board to about 2mm (⅛in) thick. Cut out the dresses using the cutter. Use the stitching wheel tool to create a broken line pattern at the neckline of the dress. Set them aside to dry on a foam pad or greaseproof paper.

2 To make the bags, roll out the blue fondant (sugarpaste) and, using the medium petal cutter, cut out several petal shapes.

3 To turn the petal shape into a bag, take a craft knife and cut away the point from the base of the petal, then cut away the circular edge. Discard these pieces of fondant (sugarpaste) so you are left with the middle section of the petal.

4 To create a handle for the bag, cut out a small oval shape from the top half of the bag. Use the stitching wheel tool to create a broken line pattern at the bottom of the bag, then set aside to dry.

5 To make the flowers, bows and bead detail, take the silicone mould and lightly dust it with cornflour, tapping out the excess. Push a small amount of softened flower paste into the mould with your finger to ensure the mould is full. If there is any excess paste spilling out of the mould, lay the blade of a craft knife on the surface of the mould and carefully cut away the excess paste, using a gentle sawing action.

6 Then turn the mould over and gently press out the decoration.

7 Apply a small amount of edible glue to the back of the decorations and fix them to the dresses and bags. For the beads, it is easier to apply the glue to the dress first, and then attach the beads.

8 Leave the dresses and bags to dry while you bake, cool and ice the mini cupcakes.

9 Apply the dress and handbag decorations to the buttercream-topped cupcakes.

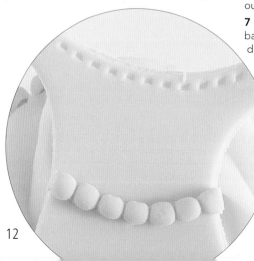

Valentine

Materials:

Mini cupcakes

Buttercream

Red, white and pink flower paste

Edible glue

Tools:

Heart-shaped cutters, various sizes

Foam pad or greaseproof paper

Instructions:

1 To make the hearts, take some flower paste and roll it out on a non-stick work board to about 2mm (⅛in) thick. Using different-sized heart-shaped cutters and different-coloured flower paste, cut out several hearts, allowing one small heart to accompany every large heart for each cupcake. Set them aside to dry on greaseproof paper or a foam pad.

2 Apply a small amount of edible glue to the back of a smaller heart and attach it to the front of a larger heart.

3 Alternatively, to achieve a more 3D effect, glue a tiny ball of flower paste behind the smaller heart and fix with glue to the larger heart.

4 Set aside the decorations to dry while you bake, cool and ice the mini cupcakes.

5 Apply the heart decorations to the buttercream-topped cupcakes.

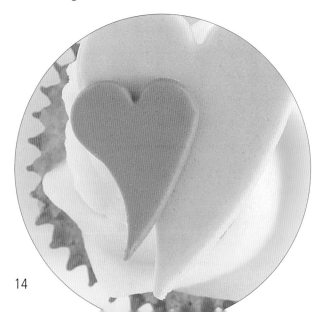

Easter Fun

Materials:

Mini cupcakes

Buttercream

Yellow, green and white fondant
(sugarpaste)

Yellow, green and white flower paste

Edible glue

Tools:

3.5cm (1⅜in) round cutter

Small and large rabbit cutters

Ball tool

Small oval cutter

Stitching wheel tool

Small star and heart cutters

Foam pad or greaseproof paper

Instructions:

1 Start by making the discs for the decorations to be mounted onto. Roll out some fondant (sugarpaste) on a non-stick work board to about 2mm (⅛in) thick. Cut out circles using the round cutter. Set them aside to dry on greaseproof paper or a foam pad while you make the decorations.

2 To make the rabbits, roll out the flower paste to about 1mm thick (¹⁄₁₆in) and use the cutters to cut out small and large rabbits. Set aside to dry.

3 Using the small end of a ball tool, make a slight indent into the base of each rabbit's body. This will hold the tail.

4 To make the rabbit's tail, roll small balls of fondant (sugarpaste), place on a foam pad and flatten slightly with your index finger. Apply a touch of edible glue to the indent made in the body and attach the tail. Repeat this for all the rabbits.

5 To make the eggs, roll out the flower paste and cut out several egg shapes with the oval cutter.

6 Before the egg shape hardens, use a stitching wheel tool to create a pattern on some of the eggs.

7 Using some rolled out flower paste, cut out some tiny stars and hearts with the small cutters. Fix these decorations to the eggs using a small amount of edible glue.

8 To assemble the cupcake toppers, apply small amounts of edible glue to the back of the rabbit and egg shapes and arrange them on the discs. Leave to dry while you bake, cool and ice the mini cupcakes.

9 Apply the decorated discs to the buttercream-topped cupcakes.

Mother's Day

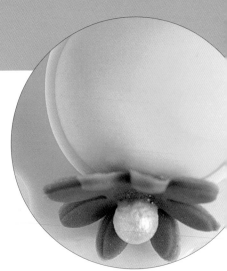

Materials:

Mini cupcakes

Buttercream

Purple, lilac and and peach fondant (sugarpaste)

Purple, lilac and peach flower paste

Edible glue

Nonpareils

Tools:

3.5cm (1⅜in) round, fluted cutter

Flower cutters, various sizes

Foam pad or greaseproof paper

Foam cupped drying tray

Craft knife

Instructions:

1 Start by making the flowers to decorate the hats. Roll out some flower paste on a non-stick work board to 1mm (¹⁄₁₆in) thick. Cut out several flowers in different sizes. It is best to have three tiny flowers to trim a hat, or one single larger flower. Place the flowers on a foam cupped drying tray to dry out. The tray shapes the petals, giving movement and dimension to the flowers.

2 The centre of the flowers can be made using a small ball of flower paste or, alternatively, a cluster of nonpareils. Either can be applied to the centre of the flowers using a small amount of edible glue.

3 To make the rims of the hats, roll out some fondant (sugarpaste) on a non-stick work board to about 2mm (⅛in) thick. Cut out fluted circles using the cutter. Set aside to dry on greaseproof paper or a foam pad.

4 Next, take some fondant (sugarpaste) and roll it into small balls with a diameter of roughly 1.5cm (½in). Place on a non-stick board and, using your index finger, slightly squash the ball into a half-sphere shape, so the underneath is flat. Make enough balls to top each of the fluted bases.

5 Apply a small amount of the glue to the centre of each base and then attach the squashed balls.

6 Next make the ribbon to trim each hat. Roll out some flower paste and, using a craft knife, carefully cut out strips of flower paste measuring roughly 3mm (⅛in) in width by 4cm (1½in) in length. The ribbon will be wrapped around the base of the squashed ball, so the length of the ribbon is dependant on the circumference of the ball.

7 Apply a small amount of edible glue to where the fluted base meets the squashed ball. Attach the ribbon and trim where necessary in order for the ends of the ribbon to overlap slightly.

8 Once the flowers have dried out, apply a small amount of glue to the back and decorate each hat around the rim (ideally covering up the join of the ribbon).

9 Set aside the hats to dry while you bake, cool and ice the mini cupcakes.

10 Apply the hats directly to the buttercream-topped mini cupcakes.

Father's Day

Materials:

Mini cupcakes

Buttercream

White, red and orange
  fondant (sugarpaste)

Edible glue

Tools:

3.5cm (1⅜in) round cutter

Star cutter, approximately
  4cm (1½in) in width

Small aeroplane cutter

Stitching wheel tool

Cocktail stick

Foam pad or
  greaseproof paper

Craft knife

Metal ruler

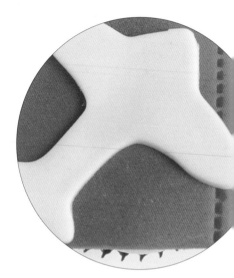

Instructions:

1 Start by making the discs to mount the ties on. Take some white fondant (sugarpaste) and roll out on a non-stick work board to approximately 3mm (⅛in) thick. Cut out circles using the round cutter. Set them aside to dry on a foam pad or greaseproof paper.

2 To make the square bases, take some red fondant (sugarpaste) and roll out on a non-stick work board to about 3mm (⅛in) thick. Using a craft knife and ruler, carefully cut the fondant (sugarpaste) into squares measuring approximately 4 x 4cm (1½ x 1½in).

3 Before the square bases dry, take the stitching wheel tool and mark a border along opposite edges of each square. Set aside to dry.

4 To make the stars, roll out some orange fondant (sugarpaste) on a non-stick work board to approximately 3mm (⅛in) in thickness. Cut out stars using the star cutter. Set aside to dry.

5 Next, make the aeroplanes using white fondant (sugarpaste) rolled out to about 2mm (⅛in) in thickness. Cut out the aeroplanes with the special cutter and set aside to dry.

6 For the ties, roll out some orange and red fondant (sugarpaste). To create the knots, use

a craft knife to cut out small squares of orange fondant (sugarpaste) measuring approximately 8 x 8mm (¼ x ¼in). Taper the edges of two opposite sides to give shape to each knot. Using a cocktail stick, gently press down into each knot to create stripes. Set aside to dry.

7 To make the tails of the ties, cut out rectangles of red fondant (sugarpaste) measuring 3.5 x 1cm (1⅜ x ½in), using a craft knife. Cut the end of each rectangle into a point. Then taper the long sides of the rectangle to give the tie some shape. Take a cocktail stick and add striped detail to the length of the tie. Set aside to dry.

8 Using edible glue, fix the aeroplanes to the square bases.

9 Fix the tail of each tie to the centre of each disc, allowing the point of the tie to overhang the disc slightly.

10 Attach a knot to the top of each tie, overlapping the top of the tail.

11 Set aside the decorations to dry while you bake, cool and ice the mini cupcakes.

12 Apply the decorations to the buttercream-topped cupcakes.

New Home

Materials:

Mini cupcakes

Buttercream

Red and blue fondant
(sugarpaste)

White flower paste

Edible glue

Edible ink colouring pen, red

Tools:

House cutter

Mini plunger flower cutter

Foam pad

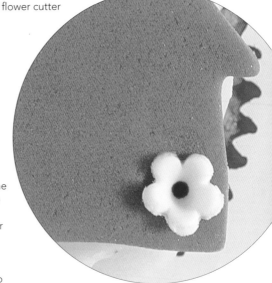

Instructions:

1 Start by making the tiny flowers. Roll out some white flower paste on a non-stick work board to approximately 2mm (⅛in) thick. Taking the mini plunger flower cutter, push down into the flower paste. Move the plunger cutter over to a foam pad and rub the cutter against the foam pad to remove any rough edges. With the plunger touching the foam pad, push the flower out into the pad. This will automatically cup the flower. Set aside on the foam pad to dry.

2 Using the edible ink colouring pen, mark a centre for each flower.

3 To make the houses, take some red and blue fondant (sugarpaste) and roll out on a non-stick work board, to about 2mm (⅛in) thick. Cut out several houses of each colour, using the house cutter, and move to a foam pad.

4 Decorate the houses with the small flowers, using the edible glue to fix them in place.

5 Set aside to dry while you bake, cool and ice the mini cupcakes.

6 Apply the decorations to the buttercream-topped cupcakes.

Halloween

Materials:

Mini cupcakes

Buttercream

Dark purple, orange, white, black and green fondant (sugarpaste)

Edible glue

White nonpareils

Tools:

3.5cm (1⅜in) round cutter

Small ghost cutter

Small bat cutter

Pumpkin cutter

Foam pad or greaseproof paper

Bone tool

Cocktail stick

Craft knife

Instructions:

1 Start by making the discs for the ghosts to be mounted on to. Take some dark purple fondant (sugarpaste) and roll it out on a non-stick work board to 2mm (¹⁄₁₆in) thick. Cut out circles using the round cutter. Set aside to dry on a foam pad or greaseproof paper.

2 To make the pumpkins, ghosts and bats roll out some orange, white and black fondant (sugarpaste) to approximately 2mm (¹⁄₁₆in) thick. Cut out the shapes in the appropriate colours and set aside to dry.

3 Before the pumpkins dry out, add definition by using a bone tool to create curved ridges.

4 To add a face to the pumpkins, take some rolled out black fondant (sugarpaste) and, using a craft knife, cut out triangles for eyes and small shapes for the mouths.

5 Shape a small amount of green fondant (sugarpaste) for the stalks of the pumpkins.

6 Attach the features to the pumpkins using edible glue. Set aside to dry.

7 To give the bats eyes, attach white nonpareils using edible glue. You may find it easier to create small indents in the fondant (sugarpaste) first with a cocktail stick for the nonpareils to sit in.

8 To make eyes for the ghosts, roll small amounts of black fondant (sugarpaste) into little balls and fix in place with edible glue.

9 Glue the ghosts to the purple discs and set them aside to dry along with the other decorations, while you bake, cool and ice the cupcakes.

10 Apply the decorations to the buttercream-topped cupcakes.

Graduation

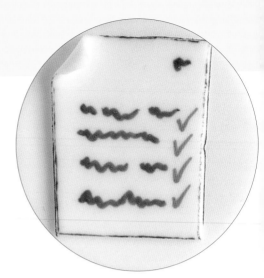

Materials:

Mini cupcakes

Buttercream

White, cream and black fondant (sugarpaste)

Red, white and black flower paste

Edible glue

Red and black edible ink colouring pens

Tools:

3.5cm (1⅜in) round cutter

Foam pad or greaseproof paper

Craft knife

Instructions:

1 Start by making discs for the decorations to be mounted on to. Take some white fondant (sugarpaste) and roll it out on a non-stick work board to approximately 2mm (⅛in) thick. Cut out circles using the round cutter. Set aside to dry on a foam pad or greaseproof paper.

2 To make the scrolls, take some cream fondant (sugarpaste) and roll into a sausage shape with a width of about 4mm (⅛in). Using a craft knife, cut into lengths of 3cm (1¼in). Set aside to dry.

3 Make the ribbon for the scroll by rolling out some red flower paste to about 2mm (⅛in) thick. Using a craft knife cut into strips measuring 3mm x 3.5cm (⅛in x 1⅜in).

4 Fix the ribbon around the centre of the scroll with a small amount of edible glue.

5 To create the exam paper, roll out some white flower paste. Cut into rectangles measuring 3cm by 2.5cm (1¼ x 1in). Slightly curl over the top left-hand corner of the exam paper and set aside to dry.

6 Once dry, take a black edible ink pen and run this around the edge of the exam paper. Add further detail to the exam paper using red and black edible ink pens.

7 For the base of the mortar board, roll a piece of black fondant (sugarpaste) into a ball with a diameter of 2cm (¾in), then use your index finger to squash the ball to create a flat surface. Set aside to dry.

8 To make the top of the mortar board, roll out some black flower paste to a thickness of 1mm (¹⁄₁₆in). Using a craft knife, cut it into squares measuring 3 x 3cm (1¼ x 1¼in). Set aside to dry.

9 Make the tassel by rolling out some black flower paste into a thin sausage shape. Cut into lengths of 3cm (1¼in). Using your index finger, flatten the end of the sausage shape. Now using a craft knife, make small slits in the flattened edge to create a tassel.

10 Assemble the mortar board by fixing the top to the base with edible glue. Then attach the tassel to the centre.

11 Attach the decorations to the discs and set them aside to dry while you bake, cool and ice the mini cupcakes.

12 Apply the decorations to the buttercream-topped cupcakes.

Christening

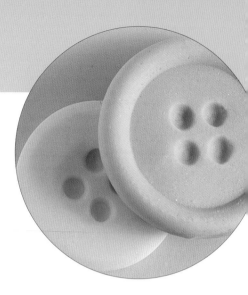

Materials:

Mini cupcakes

Buttercream

Blue, yellow and green fondant (sugarpaste)

Blue, yellow and green flower paste

Edible glue

Cornflour

Tools:

3.5cm (1⅜in) round cutter

Button silicone mould

Rocking horse cutter

Foam pad or greaseproof paper

Small paintbrush

Craft knife

Instructions:

1 Start by making the discs on which the decorations will be mounted. Take some blue, yellow and green fondant (sugarpaste) and roll out on a non-stick work board to approximately 2mm (⅟₁₆in) thick. Cut out circles using the round cutter. Set aside to dry on a foam pad or greaseproof paper.

2 To make the rocking horses, roll out some blue, yellow and green flower paste on a non-stick work board to approximately 2mm (⅟₁₆in) in thickness. Cut out the horses and set aside to dry. To assist in removing the paste from the cutter, use the end of a paintbrush to gently ease out the shape.

3 To make the buttons, take the silicone mould and lightly dust with cornflour, tapping out the excess. Push a small amount of softened flower paste into the mould with your finger to ensure the mould is filled with paste. If there is any excess paste spilling out of the mould, lay the blade of a craft knife on the surface of the mould and carefully cut away the excess paste, using a gentle sawing action.

4 Turn the mould over and gently press out the button. Make buttons in blue, yellow and green.

5 Apply a small amount of edible glue to the back of the decorations and fix to the discs.

6 Set aside the decorations to dry while you bake, cool and ice the mini cupcakes.

7 Apply the decorations to the buttercream-topped cupcakes.

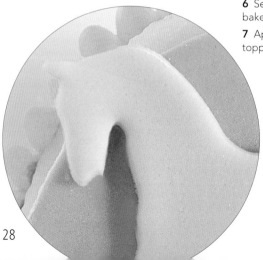

Hen Party

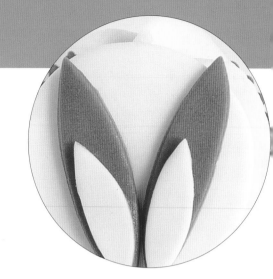

Materials:

Mini cupcakes

Buttercream

Pink and white fondant (sugarpaste)

Edible glue

Tools:

3.5cm (1⅜in) round cutter

Small wine glass cutter

Oval pointed cutters

Foam pad or greaseproof paper

Small paintbrush or small ball tool

Instructions:

1 Start by making the discs for the decorations to be mounted onto. Take some pink and white fondant (sugarpaste) and roll it out on a non-stick work board, to about 2mm (1/16in) thick. Cut out circles using the round cutter. Set aside to dry on greaseproof paper or a foam pad while you make the decorations.

2 To make the wine glass, roll out some white fondant (sugarpaste) to 2mm (1/16in) in thickness and, using the wine glass cutter, cut out several glasses. To assist in removing the fondant (sugarpaste) from the cutter, take the end of a paintbrush or a small ball tool and gently ease the wine glass out of the cutter. Set aside to dry.

3 To make the rabbit ears, roll out some pink and white fondant (sugarpaste) to about 2mm (1/16in) thick and, using the oval pointed cutters, cut out several ears. To make the inner and outer ears different colours, use the larger cutter for the pink fondant (sugarpaste) and then the smaller cutter for the white fondant (sugarpaste). Use a small amount of edible glue to attach the inner ear to the outer ear shape. Set them aside to dry.

4 To assemble the cupcake toppers, apply a small amount of edible glue to the decorations and arrange them on the discs. Leave to dry while you bake, cool and ice the mini cupcakes.

5 Apply the decorations to the buttercream-topped cupcakes.

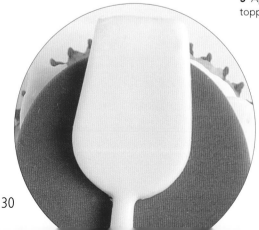

Children's Party

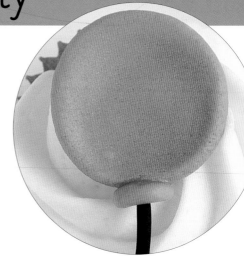

Materials:

Mini cupcakes

Buttercream

Fondant (sugarpaste)

Black flower paste

Edible glue

Food colouring paste in
colours of your choice

Tools:

Craft knife

Cocktail stick

Foam pad or
greaseproof paper

Instructions:

1 Start by making the ribbon to attach to the balloons. Roll out some black flower paste into a long, thin sausage shape with a thickness of about 2mm (¹⁄₁₆in). Cut it into lengths of 3cm (1¼in) with the craft knife. Create curves in the ribbon, making each one different, and set aside to dry on a foam pad or greaseproof paper.

2 To make the balloons, roll some fondant (sugarpaste) of different colours into balls and sausage shapes, and then flatten them with your finger.

3 To create the knot of the balloon, roll out some small balls of sugar paste and again flatten them with your finger. Apply a small amount of edible glue to the base of the balloon and fix the knot in place. Leave to dry for a short while.

4 Insert a cocktail stick into the centre of the knot and part way through the base of the balloon. Circle the cocktail stick to widen the hole slightly.

5 Apply edible glue to one end of the ribbon and insert it into the hole in the base of the balloon.

6 Leave the balloons to dry while you bake, cool and ice the mini cupcakes.

7 Apply the balloons to the buttercream.

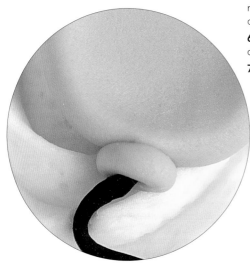

Spring Flowers

Materials:

Mini cupcakes

Buttercream

Green, yellow and lilac fondant (sugarpaste)

Green, yellow, white and lilac flower paste

Edible glue

Nonpareils

Cornflour

Tools:

3.5cm (1⅜in) round cutter

Flower plunger cutters in various sizes

Small petal cutters in various sizes

Silicone leaf veiner

Foam cupped drying tray

Foam pad or greaseproof paper

Instructions:

1 Start by making the discs for the decorations to be mounted onto. Take some fondant (sugarpaste) and roll out on a non-stick work board to approximately 2mm (¹⁄₁₆in) thick. Cut out circles using the round cutter in green, yellow and lilac. Set them aside to dry on greaseproof paper or a foam pad.

2 To make the various flowers, roll out some flower paste to about 1mm (¹⁄₁₆in) thick. Cut out several flowers in different sizes. Place the flowers on a foam cupped drying tray. The tray shapes the petals, giving movement and dimension to the flowers.

3 The centre of the flowers can be made using a small ball of flower paste or, alternatively, a cluster of nonpareils. Both can be applied to the centre of the flowers using a small amount of edible glue.

4 To make the accent leaves, roll out some green flower paste and use a petal cutter to cut out several petal shapes.

5 Before the petal shapes dry, add definition to transform them into a leaf using the leaf veiner. Dust the veiner with cornflour, and tap away any excess. Place one leaf at a time onto one side of the veiner. Place the top side of the veiner onto the leaf and gently press the two sides of the veiner together. Remove the leaf and set it aside to dry on a foam cupped drying tray. This will add dimension to the leaves in the same way that it does to flowers.

6 Once the flowers and leaves have hardened, apply them to the discs using a small amount of edible glue. Leave to dry.

7 Bake, cool and ice the mini cupcakes.

8 Apply the decorations to the buttercream-topped cupcakes.

Note: To add colour to white nonpareils, place a spoonful in a small bowl together with a small amount of lustre or blossom dust. Shake the bowl around to give the nonpareils an even coating.

Summer Delight

Materials:

Mini cupcakes

Buttercream

White fondant
(sugarpaste)

Yellow and pink
flower paste

Edible glue

Tools:

3.5cm (1⅜in) round,
fluted cutter

Small butterfly cutter

Foam cupped
drying tray

Foam pad or
greaseproof paper

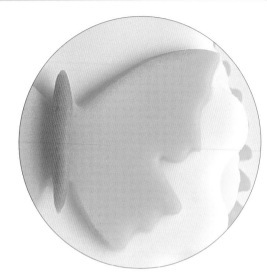

Instructions:

1 Start by making the fluted discs for the decorations to be mounted onto. Take some white fondant (sugarpaste) and roll out on a non-stick work board to approximately 2mm (¹⁄₁₆in) thick. Cut out circles using the fluted round cutter. Set them aside to dry on greaseproof paper or a foam pad while you make the butterflies.

2 To make the butterflies, roll out some yellow flower paste to approximately 2mm (¹⁄₁₆in) thick. Cut out the butterflies and set aside on a foam

pad or greaseproof paper to dry. Alternatively, leave them to dry on a cupped foam tray. This will shape the wings and give a sense of movement to the butterflies.

3 To create bodies for the butterflies, roll out thin sausages of pink flower paste, cut into lengths and apply to the centre of the butterflies using edible glue.

4 Once the butterflies have hardened, fix them to the fluted discs using edible glue. Set aside.

5 Bake, cool and ice the mini cupcakes.

6 Apply the decorations to the buttercream-topped cupcakes.

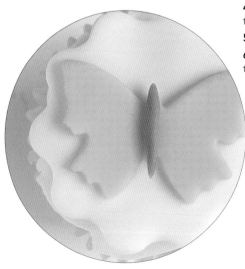

Autumn Gold

Materials:

Mini cupcakes

Buttercream

Orange, light brown and
  beige flower paste

Gold lustre/blossom dust

Cornflour

Tools:

Petal cutters, various sizes

Silicone leaf veiner

Foam cupped drying tray

Small paintbrush

Instructions:

1 To make the leaves, roll out flower paste on a non-stick work board to about 2mm (¹⁄₁₆in) thick. Cut out petals in various sizes and colours.

2 Before the petal shapes dry out, add definition to transform them into leaves using the leaf veiner. First, dust the veiner with cornflour, and tap away any excess. Place one leaf at a time onto one side of the veiner. Place the top side of the veiner onto the leaf and gently press the two sides of the veiner together. Remove the leaf and set to dry on the foam cupped drying tray. This will add dimension to the leaves.

3 In the same manner, create several more leaves in different autumn shades and sizes.

4 Using a dry paintbrush and the gold lustre dust, add highlights to the individual leaves.

5 Leave the decorations to dry while you bake, cool and ice the mini cupcakes.

6 Apply groups of the leaves to the buttercream-topped cupcakes.

Winter Warmers

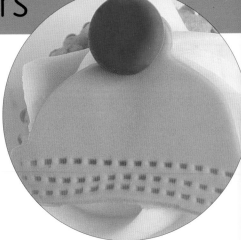

Materials:

Mini cupcakes

Buttercream

Orange, blue and yellow fondant (sugarpaste)

Edible glue

Tools:

Woolly hat cutter

Stitching wheel tool

Rolling pin

Craft knife

Foam pad or greaseproof paper

Instructions:

1 Start by making the woolly hats. Roll out some orange fondant (sugarpaste) on a non-stick work board to about 3mm (⅛in) thick. Using a cutter, cut out the hat shapes. Before the icing dries out, use a stitching wheel tool to add some detail to each hat. Set aside to dry on a foam pad or greaseproof paper.

2 To create a bobble for the hat, roll out a small piece of blue or yellow fondant (sugarpaste) and fix to the top of the hat using edible glue.

3 To make the scarf, roll out the base colour of fondant (sugarpaste) to a thickness of 5mm (¼in). In order not to have to repeat the next

steps, ensure the fondant (sugarpaste) is big enough to cut all the scarves from it at once. For eight scarves you should aim to roll out the fondant (sugarpaste) to approximately 16 x 10cm (6¼ x 4in).

4 Next, take some fondant (sugarpaste) in a different colour and roll out into a piece about 16 x 10cm (6¼ x 4in) and approximately 4mm (⅛in) thick. Cut this piece lengthways into 1cm (⅜in) strips. Remove and discard every other strip. Apply a small amount of edible glue to the remaining strips and place these on the base colour fondant (sugarpaste), leaving a gap in between each strip so the base colour fondant (sugarpaste) can be seen.

5 With the rolling pin, gently roll over the two colours in the direction of the strips. This will embed the strips into the base fondant (sugarpaste) and produce the stripes.

6 Using a craft knife, cut out scarf shapes widthways across the stripes. Each scarf should measure approximately 6 x 1.5cm (2½ x ⅝in). To add extra detail to the scarves, create frayed ends by cutting small slits into each end with a craft knife. Create a loop with each scarf.

7 Leave the decorations to dry while you bake, cool and ice the mini cupcakes.

8 Apply the decorations to the buttercream-topped cupcakes.

Wedding Day

Materials:

Mini cupcakes

Buttercream

Yellow and
plum fondant
(sugarpaste)

White flower paste

Edible glue

Cornflour

Nonpareils

Tools:

3.5cm (1⅜in) round cutter

Flower cutter

Flower veining mould

Heart cutters, two sizes

Cocktail stick

Foam cupped drying tray

Foam pad or
greaseproof paper

Instructions:

1 Start by making the discs for the decorations to be mounted onto. Take some fondant (sugarpaste) and roll it out on a non-stick work board to approximately 2mm (¹⁄₁₆in) thick. Cut out circles using the round cutter.

2 Using the pointed end of a cocktail stick, create a dotted border around each disc. Set aside to dry on greaseproof paper or a foam pad while you make the flowers and hearts.

3 To make the hearts, take some flower paste and roll out on a non-stick work board to about 1mm (¹⁄₁₆in) thick. Using the different-sized heart-shaped cutters, cut out one large heart and two smaller hearts, and attach them to the discs using edible glue. Set aside to dry.

4 To make the flowers, roll out some flower paste to about 2mm (¹⁄₁₆in) thick. Cut out several flower shapes.

5 Place one flower at a time into one half of a flower mould, which has been lightly dusted with cornflour. Apply the second half of the mould and gently push the two halves together. Remove the flower from the mould and repeat with the remaining flowers. Place the moulded flowers onto a foam cupped drying tray.

6 The centre of the flowers can be made with a small ball of flower paste or a cluster of nonpareils. Both can be applied to the centre of the flowers using a small amount of edible glue.

7 Once the flowers have dried, glue a small ball of fondant (sugarpaste) to the centre of each disc, then apply a small amount of glue to the base of the flower and push this into the ball of fondant (sugarpaste). Set aside to dry.

8 Now bake, cool and ice the mini cupcakes.

9 Apply the decorations to the buttercream-topped cupcakes.

Baby Shower

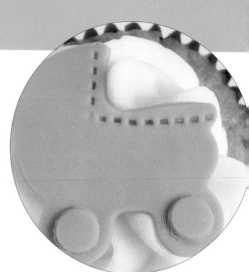

Materials:

Mini cupcakes

Buttercream

Pink, blue and white fondant (sugarpaste)

Edible glue

Tools:

Stroller (pram), bottle and bib cutters

Small star, heart and circle cutters

Cocktail stick

Stitching wheel tool

Foam pad or greaseproof paper

Craft knife

Instructions:

1 Start by cutting out the strollers (prams), bottles and bib shapes. Roll out some pink and blue fondant (sugarpaste) on a non-stick work board to about 2mm (1⁄16in) thick. Using the cutters, cut out the different shapes.

2 Before the icing dries, use a stitching wheel tool to add some detail to the strollers (prams).

3 Use the pointed end of a cocktail stick to add detail to the necks of the bibs.

4 Use the side of the cocktail stick to make indents down one side of the bottle, to represent the measuring lines.

5 Roll out some fondant (sugarpaste) and cut out some small pink hearts and blue stars to decorate the bibs. Also cut out small circles to attach to the wheels of the stroller (pram).

6 Attach the small shapes in place using a small amount of edible glue.

7 To make the nipple (teat) of the bottle, roll out some white fondant (sugarpaste) to about 2mm (1⁄16in) thick. Take the bottle cutter and cut out the top section of the bottle only. Trim away any excess paste with a craft knife so you are left with the nipple (teat) only. Glue this over the top of the existing nipple (teat).

8 Set aside the decoration to dry on a foam pad or greaseproof paper while you bake, cool and ice the cupcakes.

9 Apply the decorations to the buttercream-topped mini cupcakes.

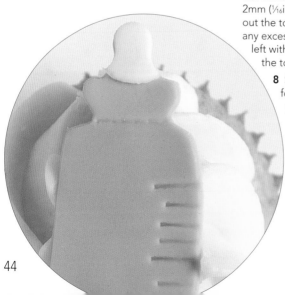

Christmas Cheer

Materials:

Mini cupcakes

Buttercream

Dark purple sparkly fondant (sugarpaste)

Dark purple and white flower paste

Edible glue

Silver lustre dust

Tools:

3.5cm (1⅜in) round cutter

Metal ruler

Craft knife

Star plunger cutters in four sizes

Veined three-leaf holly plunger cutter

Foam cupped drying tray

Foam pad or greaseproof paper

Small paintbrush

Instructions:

1 Start by making the discs for the tree and holly decorations to be mounted onto. Roll out some dark purple fondant (sugarpaste) on a non-stick work board to about 2mm (⅟₁₆in) thick. Cut out circles using the round cutter. Set aside to dry on a foam pad or greaseproof paper while you make the decorations.

2 Make the square bases in the same manner, by rolling out some dark purple fondant (sugarpaste) to a similar thickness. Using a craft knife and metal ruler, cut squares measuring approximately 3.5cm x 3.5cm (1⅜ x 1⅜in). Set aside to dry.

3 To make the Christmas trees, roll out the white flower paste to 1mm (⅟₁₆in) thick. Using the star cutters, cut out three stars in each of the different sizes. A total of 12 stars will make one tree.

4 Assemble the stars one on top of another, in descending size, fixing each one with a small amount of edible glue. Ensure the points of each star are positioned at a slightly different angle to the one below.

5 To top the Christmas tree, cut out a small star in a different colour of flower paste. Fix this to the top of the tree in an upright position using edible glue. Set aside to dry.

6 To make the holly leaves, roll out some white flower paste. Using the three-leaf holly plunger cutter, cut out several holly shapes. Place the holly leaves on a cupped foam drying tray to shape them slightly upwards. Next roll out three tiny balls of paste for the holly berries. Apply a small amount of edible glue to the centre of the holly leaves and attach the berries.

7 To make the candy canes, take a small pea-sized ball of dark purple flower paste and roll it out into a sausage shape with a length of approximately 5cm (2in) and a thickness of 3mm (⅛in). Repeat the process with white flower paste. Making the sausage shapes longer will allow you to create more than one candy cane at once.

8 Next take one end of each of the sausage shapes and push together firmly. Now with the same end firmly between your index finger and thumb, gently twist the two pieces of paste together. The more you twist, the tighter the stripe will become.

9 Once combined, place on a board and cut into lengths of no more than 4cm (1½in). Gently bend over the top end to form the candy cane shape. Set aside to dry.

10 Once the decorations are dry, apply to the square and circular bases using edible glue. To add sparkle to the decoration, take a paintbrush and gently dust with lustre dust. Leave to dry while you bake, cool and ice the mini cupcakes.

11 Apply the decorations to the buttercream-topped cupcakes.